The
Number
of Names

The
Number
of Names

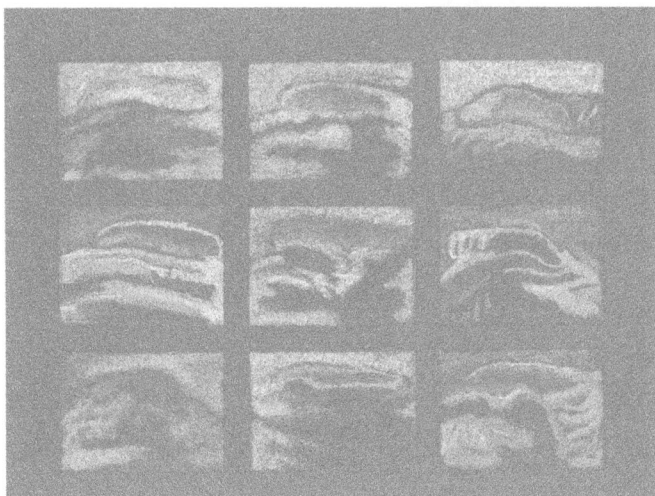

Poems

Donald Levering

SUNSTONE
PRESS

SANTA FE

Sunstone books may be purchased for educational, business, or sales promotional
use.
For information please write: Special Markets Department, Sunstone Press,
P.O. Box 2321, Santa Fe, New Mexico 87504-2321.

Book and Cover design › Vicki Ahl
Body typeface › Maiandra GD
Printed on acid-free paper
∞

Library of Congress Cataloging-in-Publication Data

Levering, Donald, 1949-
  The number of names : poems / by Donald Levering.
    p. cm.
  ISBN 978-0-86534-860-8 (pbk. : alk. paper)
  I. Title.
  PS3562.E874N86 2012
  811'.54--dc23

                                    2011051282

WWW.SUNSTONEPRESS.COM
SUNSTONE PRESS / POST OFFICE BOX 2321 / SANTA FE, NM 87504-2321 /USA
(505) 988-4418 / ORDERS ONLY (800) 243-5644 / FAX (505) 988-1025

for Jane

Contents

Acknowledgments

The author is grateful to the editors of the following publications, in which these poems, often in earlier versions and sometimes with different titles, first appeared:

The Alembic, "Descanso"
Amelia, "Blaze"
Blue Buildings, "As the Dream-Time Bees Looked On"
Buckle &, "I Came From Kansas"
Calapooya Collage, "The Effigy"
The Cape Rock, "Back Home"
Flint Hills Review, "After the Stroke"
Harwood Review, "Forest Fire"
Hubbub, "Hollows"
Icon, "Soon You Go"
Iron Horse, "Meditation at the Port"
The Lucid Stone, "The Dead Have Climbed Into My Marriage Bed,"
   "The Number of Holes," "To the Novice"
The Mid-America Poetry Review, "Mother's Donation"
Prayers to Protest (Anthology from Pudding House), "Factually Satisfied"
Prickly Pear, "Mount Mendi"
Puerto Del Sol, "Two Brothers Polishing Windows"
Quiddity, "Mother Is Moving"
Raven Chronicles, "Roadkill"
Red Wheelbarrow, "On Call"
Rocky Mountain Review, "Alterations"
Sin Fronteras/Writers Without Borders, "My Father in the Sky"
The Wisconsin Review, "All Souls' Day."

Special gratitude is due to Stephen Bunch, whose ear, encouragement, and insight have been with me from the beginning. He provided overview comments and detailed suggestions for improving this book. Also, thanks to Sheila Cowing, Robyn Hunt,

Wayne Lee, Richard Lehnert, David Markwardt, Joan Mitchell, Robert Ricci, and Barbara Rockman for their helpful comments on drafts of several of the poems. I am also grateful for the advocacy and support of Michael Scofield.

Preface

In the Kabbalah we learn that God creates the world through numbers and letters, rearranging them in infinite combinations to make new things come into being. My anthropomorphic version of this is God wearing dark glasses fingering the accordion keyboard of primal letters and numbers, playing into existence a panoply of matter and energy forms. Or God the grandfather of all fiddlers making up stories and lies to accompany the improbable songs that become our lives.

Pythagoras asserted that numbers constitute the essential nature of things. The periodic table of the elements concretizes this theory. Those of us with stakes in the creation game pay obeisance no less to recombinant DNA and the inheritance of perfect pitch than to the luck of sweepstakes and roulette wheels. What seemed to be innumerable bees flying to us from the dream-time appears to have become a finite, dwindling number as whole cultures—with their tools, their fabrics, their foods, and their epics—are consumed by the maw of human monoculture.

In the plane crash of history that we find ourselves climbing from into a place where the rivers are running upside down, all survivors are family back to Adam, back to Lucy. It is said our families are our fortunes, but are not the stars tattooing us too with their potentialities, their gifts and handicaps? Each one must retreat to the original family's sunken boneyard to plumb its dark moods. In the faces reflected on black waters we catch glimpses of our mothers and fathers, and theirs.

So the dead *are* repetitive, and we harken to them for what was, or for what we imagine their world to have been. Sometimes we bristle at what they have bequeathed us, even as we are grateful for the light of their art and science. Grandparents pass on nursery rhymes and card games as well as ethnic hatreds and pogroms. As time is circular and aunts and uncles hand down songs, we in turn confirm our children's make-belief. We follow the blazes in the trees incised by those who went before, our stricken fathers still trying to name what they see.

We need a name for the tunnel under the highway of human "progress" into the frogs' survival. We want the words to sing as we paint the bones of our ancestors. With Pythagoras, we need graphs on which to carbon-date fossilized souls. With rabbis and shamans, miners and book binders, we seek effigies to stuff with life stories, places to dwell after the piano stops ringing.

Fear of death mounts in the obliteration of an individual self merging into an Oversoul, a conversion of the matter of a single life into a prime number, a shedding of personal atoms in solar incandescence. In the light of this conflagration, we may read blind Borges affirming that the *Aleph* is the number which embraces all others. Answers are written everywhere, in the body of names that forms the world.

—Santa Fe, December 2011

I have tried to apprehend the Pythagorean power by which number holds sway above the flux.
—Bertrand Russell

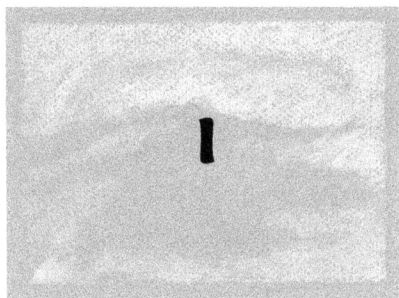

1

Meditation at the Port

Tapping his cane, calling out expiration dates,

this man with a dog
and an accordion
appears to be God handing out names.

He taps his cane on the boardwalk
and things come into being,
each with its label, each with its date of demise.

God is the blind man tapping out names.

Who knows the word for his cane?
We will call it the feeler of fate.
We will call him the maker of names.

Until my ears burn with shame,
I stare at the blind man,
thinking of things that are left unnamed.

Names for those that never escaped.
Names of *the disappeared*
are all that remain.

Thinking, does he recognize
my nervous cough? Thinking,
what is that smell on this wharf?

What is the word for his accordion?
Let us call it God's leather lung
and listen to its breathing.

Let us count its keys
that click like an abacus.
God is the blind man playing our fates.

Call his dog The One Who Discerns
A Thousand Bouquets. Nose that can tell
the overripe mangoes in crates.

But the dog names nothing
beyond her slavish longing.
Her tongue drapes her canines.

Now the blind man lifts his instrument
and with it asks where the wind begins
and when will come an end to *ethnic cleansing*.

He is told where the boardwalk ends
and where the dark waters begin.

Now he squeezes a chord
we feel in our breast bones.
Now there's a whiff of knowing.

When we stare at the blind man
we peer into our own black waters.
Is it past lives or living memory
we think we see
in the waters' wavering figures?
None know but those who see through the dark.

We think we see in English.

The blind man begins a story.
Deep in the eyeless dark swim the fish

who eat what has fallen farthest,
who swallow the names that have fallen
forever from human lips.

They mouth Muskum words for lost gods.
They move with the Singa word for "sluggishness."

Figures wavering on the water
thinking in Palumata
words from past lives
words from lost songs
words for lost tools
for carving lost gods into canoes.

Because laughter comes across the dark water
before the light of dawn.

Because we live in the wake
of big ships that pass.

Because of the sway of the stars.

Because Seru may have had the word I'm searching for.
Because of the big fish of English.

Because there is no end to the ending,
only the tapping of the blind man's cane.

Because I call myself coward
afraid to let the moment
remain unnamed.

Afraid to let the moment be.

Because at birth I accepted the gift
of eyesight
instead of feeling through dark rooms.

Because I love to loll
in the tongue of my mother and father
instead of counting in Gullah.

Because the blind man's eyelids
flutter to musicians' heaven
as he squeezes his accordion.

Because there is no ending,
only transmutation of forms.

Only the changing seascape.
Only the counting cane.

Only living inside the fog
as the waves eat the wharves away.
Living among the bickering gulls.
Swirling with midges over mangoes. Only
striving within the storm of decomposition.

Now the dark waters swallow the Wanyi names
for "becoming."

Only frog spawn and Milky Way.
Only the fish of our tongues
navigating the nameless dark.
Only incessant numbering.

Because there's no end to the naming.

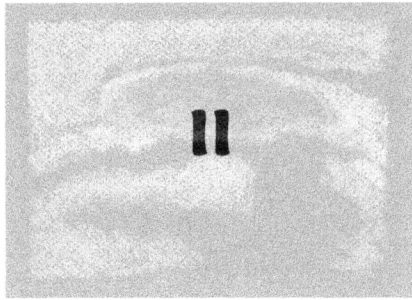

II

Blaze

for Don Lancaster

Whose axe I followed here
as an orphan trails the father
he'll never know

Faith in this braille of the bark
is all I know
leading from tree to tree

through the seasons over the summit
to this wilderness of mesquite
thorns and boulders

Hesitation
Lost among trunks
Steps retraced

I squint into the dusk
searching for the knotted hurt
feeling the bark of older trees

for the scar
that is the axe's candle
for me

and for those who follow

After the Stroke,

he, who'd taught me first words,
gets them jumbled.
Look at the cly, he says,
and indeed the clouds in the sky
are gorgeous. And we know
what he means, and so does he,
but he *just can't slay it, tamnit!*
Strangers take him for crazy
when he asks for the *mental flush*
at the drugstore, pointing to his teeth.
He tries again, *you know, the fiddle doss*,
and I recall his telling how his dad
played fiddle for weddings and wakes.
But words, not music, had been
my father's forte. He'd bought a stand,
like a pulpit, with a lamp
for his unabridged dictionary.
We'd argue over phrases
like "the Jewish race."
Now he cannot read. He starts
his tirade about the government,
and his family knows what he means
though he's reduced to sputtering.
Sometimes Mother tells him
to rest his tongue, but he will go on,
trying to name with the confidence
of a toddler. *That car is too black*,
he complains of the oncoming brights.
And he couldn't be more right.

My Father in the Sky

There you go again overhead,
regular as a weather satellite,
my lost fighter pilot
in the eternal war
against disorganization.
Before I assumed your habits,
before your elevation
to the Superego,
you blew the whistle
on double-dribblers, you called
strikes and balls, crying *Foul*
at every incivility.
When I think your windows are winking
as you bank above me,
it is really your buffed wingtips
coursing the courts of the sky.
When my barber brushes my nape,
I feel again your tickling clippers,
hear you whistling nervously
as I sit on a stool in our basement.
Your sky-writing reminds me the weave
of the Windsor knot you taught me
that I almost forgot
in my intoxication
with words you taught me,
before, in your words,
I *joined the human race*,
before the eight-to-five brown bag lunch
mortgage payments
that regulate my bowels.
Like any son who put his father down
I later boosted you

as high as Amelia Earhart,
whose legend is recounted
in the *National Geographic*
you subscribed me to.

There go the mallards overhead,
it must be autumn again.
You would be marking your scorecard,
checking our itinerary,
correcting the syntax
of wayward clouds,
directing my eyes to the sky.

The Dead Have Climbed Into My Marriage Bed

and given my jaw to our daughter.
My grandmother, who's dead,
reminds me my manners,
she passes on rhymes
I sing to my daughter.
In memory she reads to me
lists of ships from Homer.
Her handwriting hobbles across
the recipe card for her cobbler.
But bless her soul, she is merely
a mother among the ranks
whose bosses are ruthless.
They put the kibosh on dancing
with their inherited hips,
they make us solicitous
of their heirlooms,
they curse my brother
with handsomeness. Still,
Grandmother is among them,
and she tries to smooth it over
when they force her to say in my dream,
The dead don't like earphones.
They don't want us to hear
whatever they never have known,
for the dead are repetitive,
the dead don't like earphones.

The dead have given my cousin
perfect pitch, they've set
the clocks for my balding
and my daughter's menopause.
The dead recite from rote

how to bury the dead.
They hiss how to treat
a scapegoat, how to visit
vengeance in their names.
They teach us thrift, why else
would I be wrapped in Grandmother's
quilt, re-reading lists of ships?
They make me take the book
of nightmares to bed,
they cause my grandmother's voice
to repeat in my dream,
The dead don't like floor tiles.
There's no telling where they will lead,
and the dead don't like you to go
wherever they never have been.

Alterations

The tailor talks with pins
in her teeth. They slide
into a pincushion on her wrist
as she says that his inseam
measured the same as mine.

His suit still stinks of cigars
and nigger jokes. Why
did this sick uncle
choose me to will his clothing to?

Cinching the slack to my waist
she says to let out my breath.
I picture his desiccated flesh
and remove the threads of his life
bristling with our differences.

The Bus of the Dead

nears my stop at night.
Its interior lamps are lit,
so I can tell the passenger's shapes
engaged in a game of charades.
One wants the others to guess
his years shuffling paper for pay,
another mimes the pale afternoon
they closed the mill and sent him
to the unemployment queue,
a third goes through the motions
of an affair gone wrong
inside a cloud of bus fumes.
The humdrum show continues
as the bus approaches,
but then I see my father within,
and he's staring at me,
expecting me to perform
my role in the game.
Before I can finish spelling
Sweet Smell of Success,
the bus gusts past,
leaving me lying to myself.

After Father's Death, My Divorce

Boarding this plane entails the ritual
of choosing the seats, not for the usual
preferences—window or aisle,
fore not aft, away from the infant
in me, but because I know this aircraft
is taking off for nowhere,
and the seatmate who reclines

parallel with me will be the one
I remain buried beside in the sky.
I position myself in an empty row
so my fated partner
will find the seat beside me
desirable for immortality.
It's understood the plane will crash,

or already has, as we stand naked
among its remains on a broad mesa.
Some years must have passed
forward or backward,
for the airliner's traces no longer
are smoking fragments of aluminum,
but stony ruins of a theatre,

and all survivors are family.
Only after the crash do we conceive
that my father is this airplane
now lodged in thin, rocky soil,
weathering our familial dramas
with sandstone's equanimity.
Over and over my family files in

to pick their partners and seats,
over and over begins the play
I act an awkward role in.
Again and again I lose track
of the familiar plot, forget the words
of the songs and stumble in the dance,
missing the hand of my partner.

III

Forest Fire

Now listen to the noise of my heart
said my daughter by the well
in the amber light of a day
hazy with smoke.
And into the well she rolled
an enormous stone,
the boom when it hit bottom

resounding to the horizon,
becoming the hum of a swarm
of Brazilian killer bees, growing
to the roar of a forest fire
blackening the sky.
Things are no different
when I wake in a drought

to a smoky view,
the sun a crimson ball
through a black curtain,
yellow jackets swarming
outside my window,
my daughter plunged into the pipe
of burning rocks of cocaine.

That day from years ago
has returned
when I peered through the crossbar
of my swing set, hoping
to see across the yard,
but got a close-up of a hornet's nest.
My swollen eye's eclipse

turned half my world to blackness.
And I want to believe
that I didn't just hear the radio say,
between bursts of forest fire static,
The rivers are running upside down,
that every day more Brazilian rainforest
is not torched, that the Earth

is not burning down the well
of the sky, that the horizon
has not been shrunk to the view
from the rusty tailpipe
with the racketing muffler
of the crackhead's car
my daughter has climbed into.

The Number of Holes

*The portal of the sorceries one dares
not speak of*
        —Guillaume Apollinaire

That there are three doors to my home
        says it must be masculine
Odd denoting *male*
        in numerology
And having counted the nine
        holes to my body
and knowing that women have ten
        and have eaten the men's chimneys
with the mouths of their oven doors

That the rooms in my house are rectangular
        means that right angles rule
Regardless of curves in boiler
        toilet and tub
upon which our comfort depends
        In spite of the woman within
whose movements unsheathe my desires
        I declare my castle is square
and claim its kingdom for my son

That no one tallies the floor gaps
        or cracks in the plaster
in scoring the gender wars
        where a pinched nipple
equals a kick in the balls
        where the blueprint is ignored
that calls for an arch to span stressors
        where the hole for the house is single
and is bored through double hells

Hollows

Every peasant will know that there is a hollow
tree where petitions can be deposited.
　　　　　　—Fyodor Dostoevsky, *The Possessed*

And every parent or serf is aware
that this is the tree into whose hollows go
birth certificates and communion decrees.
Within these hollows is the novel
where flogged serfs believe in their God,
and the petty clerk who must log
all of Russia's aspirations
complains that his files are clogged
with ribboned locks of virgins' hair.

During the drunken naming celebrations
would any peasant forget
that the tunnel under this tree
winds hundreds of versts to arrive
through this bureaucrat's heating duct
where every pleading is stamped *rejected*?

To approach this hollow tree,
you must be led by your progeny
blindfolded into the permafrost,
you must drink the wormwood tea,
you must submit the bribe,
recite the wet-eyed entreaty.
Between your shoulder blades you must feel
the mammoth's stamp of tradition.

Entwined in your children's rites,
believing their make-belief,
succumbing to their brain fevers,

you will reinvent Christ on the rood
before their disbelieving eyes
in the wings of a butterfly.

After your daughter elopes with the anarchist,
when you're left sniffing
your wolf-boy's empty pen,
you will come to understand
the number of generations
of cruelty and boredom
that must be endured
to have your petition approved.

Purged of any purposes
save those of your descendants,
you will learn that the saint you've worshiped
has failed to grow up with your children,
that your samovar of sacrifice
has boiled itself dry,
that your master may change
but you remain chained to the estate.

Two Brothers Polishing Windows

Their parents have died
from this house, and these two
have been scrubbing reminders
of family life.
The vacuum cleaner
did nothing to remove
the vacuum—this shell
of raised dust is nothing
like their rumbling home
of a winter morning.

They team on each window,
the older brother indoors,
closer to that void
wherein their parents dwell,
the younger on the patio,
swimming against the glass.
One taps at the other's
blemishes, and the other
squeaks an erasure.

Their hands circle
the partial image of themselves,
the double glass between them
the caul of years
between their births.
Both glimpse shades
of mother or father
on the other side—
each rubs hard
to clear such sights.

My Piece of Glass

Blindfolded in the dream,
I must read a painting through my hand.
Even the heel of my hand can tell
it's the same scene again,
the picture that changes
from the frozen moment
when the jagged glass pierced his back
into the gruesome newsreel of it all
overlaid with somber music.

Close-up of my hand
that is told in the dream it must
scrape the rust-colored sorrow off
the painting with a piece
of broken glass
and make a new image,
the voice chiding I'm responsible
to turn the plot into other
than him suffering at my hand.

I hesitate to pour another,
and it all replays,
the ball I hurled over his head,
the dreadful chord of breaking glass,
the heavy fragment falling
through stretched seconds,
jabbing into his cowering back,
the pane lodged in his spine,
his legs gone forever slack.

There is no choice, I must continue
the frenzied, futile scraping

of this old painting, seizing my piece
of glass so hard my palm bleeds,
as the scene inexorably repeats,
the deformed angel of my friend down
with his single wing of glass,
not screaming, not even bleeding,
me just staring at my hand.

What my hand holds on waking
is a scar from a broken beer bottle
gained in some blotted moment,
and the certainty
I shall never grow up
to become the surgeon
who could splice his severed nerves,
I can never remake the painting
though I'm compelled to grasp the glass.

Death by Beckmann

If oil on canvas could emit sound,
the din would be as eerie
as the liquid warbling of bird-women
luring sailors to founder.
Not only does the hanging goblin
blow his horn to kingdom gone,
but inside her coffin the gaunt woman's
wide open mouth wails
her own lament.

Someone has pulled the plug
and all is muted. From a snuffed candle
in the hand of a Nubian angel
curls black smoke. A mourner
is pressed against a person-sized fish,
the rigor mortis of the painter's feeling
after his mother bedded down with cancer.
Now her green-tinged corpse submerges
in the satin sheen of her shroud.

In the upper room where Faith
would picture a stage for the Hereafter,
where an appeasing German
would paint his mother in chorus
with Aryan seraphim,
Beckmann's loss expresses
looming cuttlefish.
His three tuxedoed brothers howl
from the sheet music of cicadas.

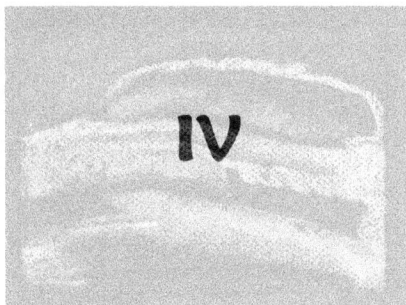

IV

On Call

A flock of birds stretches above the water
as I walk the beach dialing my daughter
The blinking foghorn on the jetty
sounds the darkening sea
before my call reaches her

not expecting me
for she's the on-call mortician
this holiday weekend
Somebody's got to do it
Deaths do not conform
to a clockwork factory god
but wash up in waves after hours

She reports a spell of low mortality
People haggle sneeze seduce guffaw
blow up balloons for birthday parties
sing the obligatory song
Then the tide will shift
bodies will crowd my daughter's roster
to be bagged and removed

Before hanging up we joke
that in the end
she will take care of me
We repeat the joke
until we believe it

African elephants signal each other
in sounds too low for human ears

Through the ground comes the call
to come to the funeral
of one of their fallen
They drop the branches from their trunks
stop spraying each other in watering places
or rouse from naps
and start marching across the savanna

April 29th, 1720
                                a voice in a dream
warned the Viceroy of Sardinia
of the coming plague
He turned away the *Grande-Saint-Antoine*
before it could drop anchor
But cholera had already slipped in
Among the first to succumb were morticians
Streets became clogged with corpses
gnawed by rats and dogs
Smoke from putrid pyres rose
with crows lifting pieces to the sky

In my dream the fear is
the darkness inside
the bell of a tuba
A whole band of them marching up the hillside
their tones deep as the signals of elephants

Even more terrible
the tubas silent
in procession down a flowering hill
Threads of spittle dripping from mouthpieces

I can no longer see the passing birds
after the call to my daughter
Sand pipers in the last light
skitter just ahead of me
The chill water soaks my pantslegs
I feel the tug of the undertow

Someone has to do it
Has to enter the dreaded room
        don a mask that does not stop the smell
                gloves that cannot shield the grievers

Somebody has to be on-call
to pick up the body
Someone has to signal
for the loved ones to gather

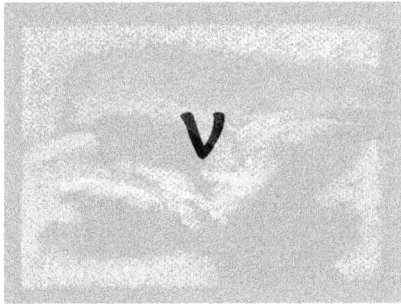

As the Dream-Time Bees Looked On

an Anbarra burial ritual,
six years after the death

It began before time and grieving

with the honeybee song
and two logs

The log that had housed the honeybees' hive
was sanded smooth
It became the funerary log

The other log was imagined
then sculpted from sand
while the kangaroos looked on

Now the honeybees had swarmed
from the funerary log
just as the life had flown
from these burial bones

And imaginary bees
from before there was time
flew in a line
to the sand-sculpted log
with nectar for the spirit
of the dead man

The wind songs began
And the faces of the winds
were painted on both ends
of the funerary log
And the bones to be buried

were rubbed with red ochre
as the red ochre song was sung

And the painting of the log went on
with the plover and the plover song
the gannet and the gannet song
the turtle and the turtle song
until the log was painted all over
with spirits from the place before time

Then the live men were painted white
and the diggery-dos were blown
as the dead man's ochre bones
were clutched by white crow dancers
and stuffed into the burial log

Inside the crow dancers' limbs
swarmed the imaginary bees
And the painters carried the log
while the diggery-dos were blown

and the white crow song was sung
And the mourners snaked through the dunes
to the beach from before time began

where the log was raised and planted
and the spirit of the dead man

rushed down under the sea

Mount Mendi

after Dogan myth

Evenings the sun drops
into Mount Mendi,
dome of abundant copper
three days' hike away.
Souls of the dead are taken there
crowded in a wagon
so say travelers
who have watched them pass
like potted blue gentians
nodding on a racket of wheels.
Witnesses vow that the driver's skin
changes hue like burning coals
as the wagon winds
through Mendi's foothills.
A few have glimpsed
the driver's foxfire form
tipping the cart at the switch-
backs, letting the blue flames
of souls fall to choosing
among fossils left from the Flood.
The lucky ones find the curve
of a dolphin's fluke
or webbing of kingfisher's wings.
The other souls continue the climb
to the great charnel house
where they are turned into copper
when the sun is lifted
by black birds.

The Effigy

Celtic Ritual

It begins with the cleaning of ditches
when someone finds the remains
of a badger or boar
that died in a winter storm.
A witch is summoned
to consign the animal's soul
to the bundle of last year's straw
stuffed in a shirt and trousers.
Then it's paraded to town,
where it's burned on a pyre
to applause and hurrahs.
Fiddles and bodhrans strike up
the refrain that everyone joins
during countless rounds:
His blizzards are gone to the blossoms
His sniffles dispersed by the bees.
The effigy's coals are brought
to the newlyweds' hearth,
its ashes strewn on young graves.
Now begins the plowing under
of last year's stubble,
the sowing of peas
till shoulders are sore.

All Souls' Day

The pumpkins on porches have begun to go to grimace
as I turn the corner and kerosene smoke
twists into my nose

before the iron spheres appear,
guarding the open grave
of a broken gas line.

Dodging black puddles, I look up
at a cawing crow
and slip on pumpkin guts.

Cold slushwater seeps through the seam in my sole,
soaking my sock, the way Grandfather's limp
sought him autumn evenings.

Removal

When the call comes,
the two find the address and squeeze inside.
Nearly a hundred, the woman guesses,
crammed into the tiny home,
loud with waves of mourning,
pungent from living bodies
and the one they had come to remove.
The clinging grievers would not budge
to let the pair through.
The room is so close it seems to her
as if their ancestors huddle here too.
A few words in their language
over and over by the man,
the woman's insistent nudging,
and at last they push through to the bed.
Clad in long black, hired criers
crowd the deceased, ululating
like other-worldly birds,
raising the pitch of all of the others.
Deftly the two elbow them aside,
wrap the rigid man and lift him to go,
but this triggers histrionics;
the volume of protests grows
almost liquid as they wade through
the clutching hands and shrieks of disbelief,
making their way with their burden toward the door.

Lima Subterranean

Beside the Rio Rímac, the clanking
jaws of the construction crane
expose an ancient wall.
Excavation for the high-rise
is halted.
Careful shovels unearth
the rest of the pueblo's ruins
overlooking the river.
Roofless rooms seem so small
to have held generations'
birthday songs, wedding feasts,
mourners keening.
Potsherds are sifted from the dirt
and stored in archaeologists' bins.

Near Plaza Mayor, peeling frescoes
along the monastery portico
reveal paintings over paintings—
the flaking blue of the Virgin's robe,
a bleaching angel's wing,
a hand with an eye in its palm.
Underneath their holy dwelling
Franciscan brothers welcomed
the remains of the faithful.
Family after family gained
final residence in the twisted
tunnels until the space
no more could contain
single graves, so the brothers
began to stack the corpses

between sand and lime,
six layers deep in time.
Through plagues and earthquakes
families still demanded
safekeeping under the church.
The brothers built receptacles
and dismantled skeletons
to store tibias with tibias,
hipbones nestled like ladles,
spines with spines like giant seahorses
swimming in their dusty bins
so that more could be welcomed in.

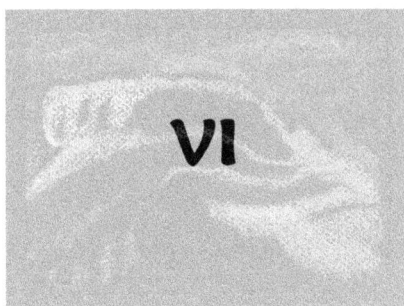

VI

The Death of Our Buddha

on all fours as a Labrador befell
as Borges and his consort lofted
over vineyards in a balloon.

Buddha's heart had been filling with fluid
even as he was bounding to the pond
clamped on a stick the size of a man's

femur, leaping after looper moths
and floaters in his eyes, the first signs
of terminal detachment.

On his return from the pond,
he simply stopped wanting.
By evening his breaths were numbered.

His heart with its ocean had grown
too large for this incarnation.
In candlelit vigil his soul escaped.

The dog's owners declared
a decade of mourning.
They stopped the remodeling.

Now that our retriever has passed,
they asked, *how can we complete
the Temple Sagrada Família?*

The grief of the world was commensurate.
The Dalai Lama's retreat
was cut short.

Stock exchanges plummeted
with the uncertainty
of Buddha's release from the cycle.

At the Labrador's funeral Borges
read to us about the one number
encompassing all others.

But who, we wondered, will show us
how to relinquish our gravity?
From where, we despaired,

will come our boundless compassion?

Hideo Manifested

Hideo is a candle flickering all night
in green glass placed
over his own grave.
Something has broken
his perfect body, Hideo
is no longer in pain.
A body broken deeply enough
becomes water, becomes torrent.
His namesake was a peacemaking man
from Japan reborn in feline form.
When Hideo makes the rounds rubbing legs
he brings all parties together.
With his plush fur and throaty purring
he absorbs the atom bomb.
Consummate hunter Hideo
catches moths mid-flight,
brings home lizards and mice,
prairie dogs, rabbits,
gazelles, elk, tusked boars.
He toys with his stuffed dolphin.
Terror of birds, he is up
in the trees springing at them,
sprinting across the roof to leap.
Easy to see him as panther,
but when he returns,
Hideo's a percussionist,
a dark and lively little man
who never stops drumming,
Zapateo dancing, his feet
thumping the floor.
Finally he drops asleep, his little
blast furnace roaring

within his blue grey fur.
Hideo beds with our restless legs,
curving to nestle my chest.
When he wakes, Hideo
jumps his playmate, sparring with him,
and when they lie down together,
he grooms him with his tiny pink tongue.
He asks to drink from the bathtub faucet
because he is to become
a purling body of water.
But something has broken
Hideo's perfect body,
his femur is cracked,
his pain unthinkable.
Something that crushes and maims
has turned him from hunter to prey.
In the season of marigold blooms,
something has unmade him.
As he lies in his grave Hideo becomes
a curving fjord, sleek and smooth,
his deep waters moving through bedrock.

Cramp

Eighty-five years this day
since my father's face
contorted into a cry
for first breath

and more than a year
since his final grimaced
mute mouthings
the hospice worker said

were merely spasms
from the nerves that work the jaw
though what I saw was father trying
to call his fear

Today I woke remembering him

after the dream of reaching
to unclench my toes
from a cramp
my body forming an O

Hard work this prying
Hard giving voice to his open mouth
that mimed howling
as the locusts shrilled outside

Not easy
making out his meaning
that I sometimes hear
as NO! NO! NO!

to leaving behind what he loved

Memorial Day

Flags up and down the street
as the Air Force of little beetles
devours the leaves of my grape vines.

In their miniature mouths each leaf
becomes a delicate lacework
until only veins are left,

leathery sluiceways
that are nothing so much
as my skeletal father at the end.

He had loved to dollop
spoonfuls of jelly on toast.
His favorite, gooseberry,

grew on vines like grapes,
but had the tang of his father's
bawdy fiddle tunes.

Dust of the beetles' waste
lifts in the breeze that carries
patriotic fanfares from the town square.

Deserting my decimated vines,
the beetles swarm my neighbor's flag
taking with them

autumns of jellies and wines.

Mother's Donation

On the airplane I'm reading about radium,
how it sheds electrons
in luminous decay.

In Mother's day nobody knew
the whole story
of radium's fluorescence.

Workers who painted clock hands
moistened the tips of their brushes
and later lost tongue and esophagus.

I arrive to find Mother more like Lear,
writing the names of my sisters
on undersides of china and furniture.

Donating hours with hospice patients
isn't enough.
She has given her brain to Science.

Every month she visits clinicians
who measure her grey matter.
I don't need a scale to tell the changes.

In her apartment I lie awake
staring at the glowing hands
of her clock with my name on the bottom.

Before the Columbarium

In her grief a dozen years ago
she'd thought she'd soon be freed
to join her husband. *Instead*,
she tells her son, *I'm still stuck here.*

Less and less she slumbers, turning over
the vagaries of disease or habits
through which her family members
go. The way loved ones disappear,

it feels like Stalin's reign again.
When she finally falls asleep, the orphans
roaming Moscow's railway stations
beseech her once more.

The rising sun, immortal tyrant,
runs his finger down his list
of fatal ailments, ticking off
one of her friends after another.

Global news is more and more remote.
Families losing all in Wall Street swindles,
houses swallowed by thawing permafrost,
Kremlin mafia fêted in Washington.

Nothing she can conceive or mend
with a kiss like a son's scraped knee.
It all just makes her weary.
She pats his father's faceplate,

*Spats we had, but he was generous
to you boys and loyal to me.*
She rubs the vacant chamber adjacent,
affirming to her son, *This is where I'll be.*

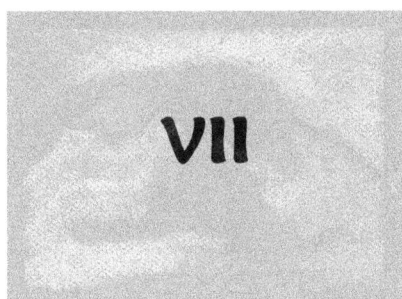

VII

Father's Visits with Gladys

Before the conflagration on a cake
Father Shogren speaks the blessing
at Gladys' birthday celebration.
Phrases he recites are not
the ones reeling in his mind
mixed with Meister Eckhart's.

Bring your restless mind to me.
I will help you simplify
Cries the maggot fly.

She mostly remembers who is who,
though what was spoken moments ago
has vanished quick as the balloons
her great grandchildren keep popping
without a sound to Gladys.
The kids lick a hundred candles clean.

His smiles do not betray his thoughts:
God is the grand amnesia,
The all-absorbent blotter,
Abyss between the molecules
Into which all
That was
Falls.

Father finds her in a different room.
Nothing and no one familiar to her.
She refuses to stay within,
wheels herself up and down the hall.

Concludes it's all a ruse, finds herself
back in Bergen, cheerful rainy days
with a musical husband
in a new apartment.

All of creation cannot keep God company.
For God wishes to be alone
In the space between stars.

Saguaro sentries in the gravel yard
when Shogren comes with Eckhart under arm.
"Yesterday Papa took me to the creek.
Wish you could have been there," she says.
"Warm breezes and buzzing dragonflies
and water striders dimpling the surface.
Over and over Papa cast his line,
the sun shone bright on slick rocks,
the water rippled over boulders..."

Each moment holds the fruit
Of all that is past
And the seeds of all that will be.

"...and from the rippling stream
very slowly there seemed to lift—
how do I say it—a chain
of hexagonal light. Yes, I said
hexagonal, I'm not dead yet.
Above the surface hovered
this chain of hexagonal light.
What did you say your name was?"

What piece of the puzzle can the All
Do without?
Without everything, the One is nothing.

Next visit she's fidgety and cross.
"It's unseemly the way they treat me.
Pills to make me stop talking.
Interrupting Mother's visit
with their routines.
The cleaning woman turning on
the idiotic TV.
Orderlies prodding me to pee
as if I were a toddler."

If everything is foreordained
How hoarse is the chorus of seraphim?

Her visitor reads to her from Psalms,
listens to her state her plight.
"They don't see me through the drooling,
haven't a clue who I am.
I am my only husband's second wife.
I am the mother of three.
One of these has gone on
before me."

The world is comprised of innumerable ones.
One angel doth deny he is another.
The Devil's invitations
Include everyone.

This visit she's bright as a finch.
Repeats that she went to the creek.
Speaks about the leafy breeze,
the jeweled dragonflies,
and fishing with her father.
Again her awe with the rising
honeycomb of light.
Remembers Father Shogren's name.

From the single spark
Of an angel there springs
All that is green and leafy.

"Yes, I have regrets.
I tolerated fools I should have shunned.
But more than stewing
I have wonder.
Was meeting Tom that Sunday afternoon
inevitable? Yes I said
inevitable, I'm not yet dead.
Sometimes I hear Tom's mellow bass again.
We shared such pleasure singing duets,
time would come unhinged."
Her guest hears salsa from the nurses' station.

Can Being be without the flesh,
Without the crystal machinery?

VIII

Riderless Horse

The undertaker paints your face
with yellow paste, then draws
a line around your neck.
You're not planning to slit my throat?,
you ask, and when he answers,
Yes, so hushed, you realize
he doesn't want others to hear,
your still being alive
is an inconvenience.
That's when you see your family
signaling you to keep still
and let the mortician finish you off.
After all, they're already grieving.
You swear you will never permit
these balding women and gimpy men
to escort <u>you</u> in perfect health
to your grave.
So you leave through the arbor
on the riderless horse
as everyone stares, still wearing
the paste on your face,
tornadoes forming in yellow sky.
You try to sit taller
but keep sinking into the horse,
struggle, breathing hard,
and finally succumb,
becoming one
with the riderless horse.

To the Novice

Find the grace you crave
in turning the compost,
consolation in digging
your sister's grave,
patience waiting
for the lilac cutting
to bud.
Raise your eyes
to the trolling satellites,
listen to the snapping prayer flags.
Know that hemlock roots
have written in rock
that the body takes
four years to decompose,
three to migrate
to Earth's core,
countless more to convert
from matter to prime numbers.
Rest from your intentions.
Let the locust and the dove within
awake.

Factually Satisfied

You know the weight of your soul
and how it will fly toward the sky's center.
You have burned with the smudgepots against the frost
and have stored the strata of music you've heard.
Within are the persons who mothered or fathered you,
your feelings and organs and hymns.

Before you go, you can unbind from gene
and ritual, you can release
your recurring nightmare
into the Oversoul.
You can unlearn the spells of stars
and let go of your echo.

Soon You Go

There is no withdrawal
from the envelope of sky,
no diving to Earth's core.
No proof for faith; no painless
suicide. Only the sliding
musical phrase, as time
releases you in its time.
Even when diffused to the sky
as smoke, or reduced
to a box of bones
leaching into earth,
the universe uses facts
to make you *you*.
Not an anchored ship in harbor,
not a diamond-studded drill
homing in on wisdom,
you are more like a spoon
that is used to ladle rose water.
Though you dance with abandon
to fiddle and drum,
tomorrow you may writhe
on the pyre of harvest sacrifice.
You see your image on a pond,
your will in a vein of iron ore,
your children in hills
of blackberry bramble.
But in the basement of being
you are blind. Soon you go
to mineral and ash, soon
to the carbon of stars,
to the marrow of Earth,
soon to your body of words.

I Came From Kansas

       from a moment
of my parents' passion,
       from furrow and corn pollen,

earthworm and wheat wagon.
       From Orlando's fiddle
and Elsie's hymnal

       I descended.
I keep arriving every time
       the Santa Fe railroad blows through.

My movement through my mother's womb—
       no more important than a blue jay's squawk,
no less enduring than grandchildren's genes

       stored in my daughter's ovaries.
From flour and yeast I rise
       and follow my father's passage

through the tomb
       past Venus past Mercury,
and am consumed.

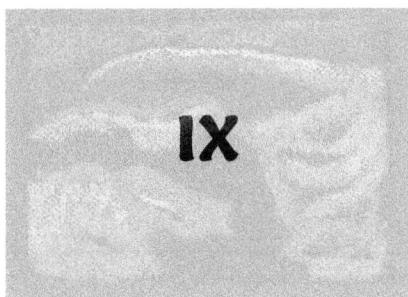

IX

Mountainside Memorial

for Robert Saenz (1977–2006)

We who have convened in formal black
           or chains and Gothic makeup
to witness the scattering of your ashes
           in this place that remembers
your campfire revelry
           picture you in cape and beret
hoop earring and panther tattoo
           taking us all in with your waggish grin

As vapor rises
           from these sunlit snowdrifts
your father's minister asks us
           to bow our heads
admit we are sinners
           pronounces his belief
that once you did receive *Jesus*
           so on that glorious day to come
you will be lifted away
           from the unfaithful

If something of you can hear our thoughts
           can sense intention
beyond these trappings
           of faith and denial
can feel us bowing
           to the lord of leukemia
to the loyalty of lovers and friends
           who have gathered for you in these pines
to see your ashes blow away
           and remain

Descanso

When the hair on the back of my neck
signals a lightning-strike,

when two star-struck cars
take aim for a head-on.

Because my hands turn up and open
to pinpricks of starlight

and then turn down to pick up
windshield fragments on the road.

That my fingertips fill with slivers.
That her bloodstains on the pavement

deepen before they bleach away.
Because the needles from roadside pines

keep on falling every season,
because the needles continue to fall.

Now that a cross marks the curve
where the crash occurred.

Now that the highway's shoulder
is turning to pine-needle mulch.

Roadkill

for Sandy

Braking quickly, my daughter
steers to the shoulder.
She dons gloves and carries a bag
to harvest the raccoon
she will bury in her backyard.
From wherever they dwell
maggots are summoned.

Under rocks and dirt in my dream
there churns a dark combustion
of beings who consume
and in turn are consumed

I reach into the great furnace
of winter and sleep
to remove each brittle word
and place it on the sill to cool

As I merge into traffic
red eyes reflect—I stomp
the brake pedal and swerve.
My car wobbles,
almost toppling, halts.
Behind, another car's ugly thud.

Returning next day I ponder
that animal's chances

of making it across
eight lanes of glaring reflections,
the tons of noise bearing down
on one small possum.
How deftly between passing cars
the ravens feed on its carcass.

Car bomb, land mine, roadkill
Skunk, squirrel, cat, shepherd
Soldier, potter, father, daughter

In Tennessee there is a tunnel
under a highway
for the springtime frog migration.
For this we need a word.

Weeks later she exhumes the raccoon
brushes off the dirt to find
the maggots have cleaned the skull
of all flesh and left it smooth.

What large eye sockets
to take in the night.
How tiny the bones in its paws.

In her room she places its skull on her sill
between the cat's and the squirrel's.
She lights a candle before it
and pictures the raccoon by moonlight
cleaning its food in a stream.

Back Home

for my mother

Rolling over hummocks of drought-struck corn,
we pause before the crossing—motor dimmed,
dry husks rustle in the wind
and the rails moan
from a train still miles away.
A redbird whistles.

We coast into the cemetery.
The markers stretch to the corn rows.
Spider webs shake in parched trees
as your words ride a warm breeze
showing where our ancestors lie
near Grandfather's buried urn.

Back on this side of the tracks,
we stop to watch the train blow past.
In its wake you speak
of your father's soul
and the wheat cars click
across the belly of the land.

Crossing the Footbridge

over black waters, beneath me floats
the specter of Grandmother's racked face.
A few paces more, and I wade into
the overgrown family graveyard—
eroded names of miners, tanners,
grocers, gleaners, and book binders
on mossy headstones in a topsy-
turvy seascape of sunken graves.

I imagine instead I'm strolling through
manicured Eternity Acres,
where all would behold my noble
ancestors' monikers emblazoned
on marble mausoleums with emblems
as magnates, judges, and founders.
Among them would be flower-strewn
shrines for the beatified,
perpetual flames flowing.

My pioneer kin's wild whiskers
would be trimmed with the lawns,
the women's menses-stained bloomers
would be bleached and raised
as sails on cumulus schooners
chartered from my forebears.
On the high ridge of the memorial grounds
my undying mother would plant vines
that escape the family plots to cover
these coal-gouged hills with ambrosial fruits.

That gossip about the arson
of Grandfather's shop, the whispering

behind Grandmother's dark moods
would convert to veneration.
Mapmakers would measure my stride
and give my name to a boulevard.
I can hear it now—the people saying
There goes the scion of that honorable line,
as I recross the bridge into town.

Returning to My Grandparents' Place

It's smaller than in memory
And the hedge that defined its corner lot
is gone into a scar along the sidewalk

The shady elm now a stump awash in glare
Grandmother's irises smothered in lawn
Widened driveway over Granddad's vegetable patch

This time I don't get sent to the legless veteran
propped in his bed
with cupcakes from our family

This time I don't drop the blue jay
from the yew with my BB gun
and the nestlings don't cheep themselves to death

Looking in I recall my Grandmother
reading to me of Odysseus
returning disguised as an aged beggar

But all is to be flooded
behind the great dam of Kansas–
Granddad's tomatoes ripening on the sill

the cards laid for King-on-the-Corner
the village of knickknacks on the mantle
that used to be part of my hands—

all to be floated away

Reunion

Each wrong turn brings them closer.
Her youngest son's behind the wheel
in a city whose streets he merely
knew as vague surroundings
to the backseat with his teddy.

The signage is obscure; the map
to suburban family reunion
slides from her lap to the floorboard.
He senses they're straying from
their destination, an uncanny
wind blowing them toward
a place that's disappeared,

as they peer from bridges
and round a cloverleaf
to find themselves rolling down
a ramp into inner city.
They drift past Polish beer halls
and Spanish laundromats,
weathered brick and wooden houses.

Then she was being driven fast
in labor for her first son
decades ago to this
boarded-up hospital
they are coasting past.
The stone church she'd worshiped in
long before goes by their windows.

Halted at a red across from
Talisman Tattoos, the son gawks

at a huge woman breast-feeding
a toddler by a beauty shop.
A cracked hipster on the corner
cries for his lost porpoise, warns
of deaths to come.

None of this can budge the mother
from her compass in that scorching summer
before air conditioning, sleeping
with other families outside for the breeze
in the park they now are passing,
where signs flutter
for another reunion.

Mother Is Moving,

giving all away to live her last days
as a saint on a rest home's top floor.
To the poor she donates sweaters,
rolling pin, picture frames. To the hospice
goes the furniture of a sturdier age—
oak bureau, rocking chair, grandfather clock.
To my daughter, wafer-thin heirloom spoons—
the republic of memory's coins melted down
into curvatures of nourishment.
If anything is mean in her, it will be in my bones.

At dawn on her final day in her own home
Mother is reading her Bible.
Through the words of Paul she is traveling the highway,
passing beggars, soldiers, confidence men,
a tax collector spying from a sycamore,
one generous husband. In ninety-one years
she has seen all the apostles and devils
going down the road. Her bags are packed
with private things, she waits for the taxi.
If anything is ungrateful in her, it will be in me.

To my brothers have gone Father's golf clubs
so they may turn into cranes on the links.
To me was bestowed Dad's skinny bird legs.
From her high window mother looks out
on the world spinning away from her
as her own body begins to go.
Yesterday it was her sore shoulder,
this morning a forgotten word.
We are all flying from home.
If there be any sadness, it will be mine.

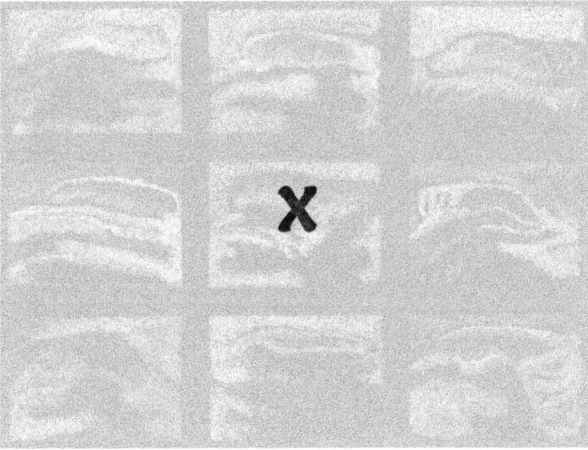

The Number of Names

The clicking of the abacus of grief
strapped to the calves of refugees
The ratio of crutches to land mines
The long division of famine

The pennies on dead men's eyes
The dollars fed into slot machines
Repeating zeroes of Ferris wheels

The number of knots in the net for the cannon-shot acrobat
The tonnage of bombs dropped on Iraq
The rate of exchange of souls for petroleum

Water for the butterfly bush
Sounds of running water

Rounds of sea glass rosary beads
Turns of prayer wheels in Himalayan breezes
Heads bowing toward Mecca

The four letters of the genetic alphabet
The litter of cloned sheep
The census of missing butterflies
The number of syllables in a groan
The twists in the history of a dust mote

Wind that disperses blessings and hymns
Wind blowing pollen and pheromones

The three denials of the crowing cock
The five lambs sacrificed to a ram-headed prophet
The eleven devils dancing on the masks of avarice

The tally of grains of grass on the back of an ant

The hundred million molecules in a breath of the Buddha
The number of unenlightened humans

Wind stiffening a wind sock
Wind in the rushes and leaves
Sounds of rushing wind

The Dispensation of Randomness in the gnats' dance
The chance of a living planet between lava and ice
The number of kidney stones paving the path to Paradise

The number of stars in the visible sky
The number of stars invisible
The number of digits for Pi
Numbers for the letters of the names for Yahweh
Their totals which can never be told

Water that cleans as it flows
Wind that freshens old sheets
Wind that whistles through bones

The number of water droplets in a bog
Inscrutable ciphers of worms
The sum of frogs on the road to extinction
The total acres of styrofoam
The four thousand eight hundred sixty-two rings
in the stump of the bristlecone pine

The number of manta rays circling the seven seas
The weight of the sublimated snow
The names for the notes of the water flute
The data dance of bumblebees

Water that cleans as it falls
Wind that disperses crematory smoke

The number of eggs between puberty and menopause
The number of spermatozoa in twin testicles
Reductive equations of lust

Wind that stirs the grasses and flags
Water that rolls over boulders
Water that smoothes over edges

The number of boxcars boxcars boxcars
Octaves of blackberry canes
repeating themselves to the sea
The length of the aria's vowels
The depth of childhood scars

The stitches in Grandmother's quilt
The number of kisses per minute
The number of consonants in laughter
The lucky lottery number
The promises attributed to God

Notes

"Meditation at the Port"

> *The disappeared (los desaparecidos)* refers to persons associated with resistance to repressive regimes who have been abducted. Often these individuals are never seen again.
>
> Muskum is an extinct language once spoken in Chad; Singa in Uganda; Palumata in Indonesia; Seru in Malaysia. Gullah is an endangered language spoken by descendants of African slaves on islands off the coast of South Carolina and Georgia; Wanyi is an imperiled Queensland aboriginal tongue.

"My Father in the Sky"

> George Burns Levering worked for Trans World Airlines for forty years and moonlighted as a sports official.

"Forest Fire"

> The opening dream was appropriated from a dream recorded by Sir Edward Burne-Jones in *The Gates of Horn and Ivory*, compiled by Brian Hill.

"On Call"

> An account of the plague of Sardinia is related in Antonin Artaud's "The Theatre and the Plague."

"All Souls' Day"

> Before the days of electric blinking construction barriers, travelers were warned of ground hazards by black, kerosene-fueled lamps about the size of a bowling ball.

"Lima Subterranean"

> Tens of thousands of the faithful are buried in the Catacombs of the Church of San Francisco.

"The Death of Our Buddha"

> Edwin Williams' biography of Jorge Borges includes a photograph of the Argentinian author in a balloon gondola with María Kodama in the Napa Valley.
> Antoni Gaudí's grandiose Temple Sagrada Família in Barcelona remains unfinished after over a century of nearly continual construction.

"Father's Visits with Gladys"

> Quotations from Meister Eckhart are found in his *Essential Sermons*.

"Mother Is Moving"

> This poem is written after Cesar Vallejo's "Los pasos lejanos."

About the Author

Born in Kansas City, Donald Levering was educated at Baker University, The University of Kansas, Lewis and Clark College, and Bowling Green State University in Ohio. At Bowling Green, he was a Devine Memorial Fellow in Poetry before receiving a M. F. A. in Creative Writing. He has worked as a human services administrator, computer operator, free-lance journalist, groundskeeper, and teacher in the Diné (Navajo) Nation.

In addition to wide appearances in literary journals, his publications include five chapbooks of poetry, *The Jack of Spring* (Swamp Press), *Carpool* (Tellus), *Mister Ubiquity* (Pudding House), *The Fast of Thoth* (Pudding House), and *The Kingdom of Ignorance* (Finishing Line Press), as well as three full-length poetry volumes, *Outcroppings From Navajoland* (Diné College Press), *Horsetail* (Woodley Memorial Press), and *Whose Body*, (Sunstone Press).

Mr. Levering was a recipient of a National Endowment for the Arts Fellowship Grant in poetry and won first place in the Quest for Peace (rhetoric) Writing Contest. He was an Academy of American Poets Featured Poet in the online Forum. Father of a daughter, Sandy, and son, Nate, he lives with the artist Jane Shoenfeld in Santa Fe, New Mexico.

www.ingramcontent.com/pod-product-compliance
Lightning Source LLC
Chambersburg PA
CBHW031143090426
42738CB00008B/1198